Made in the USA
Coppell, TX
08 March 2021

51448128R00061